THE
**FACTS
ABOUT**

Cults

by Sarah Stevens

CRESTWOOD HOUSE

New York
Maxwell Macmillan Canada
Toronto
Maxwell Macmillan International
New York   Oxford   Singapore   Sydney

LIBRARY OF CONGRESS CATALOGING-IN-PUBLICATION DATA

Stevens, Sarah.
    Cults / by Sarah Stevens.—1st ed.
        p.   cm. — (Facts about)
    Includes glossary/index.
    Summary: Discusses the nature and methods of cults and the effects they have
on those who become involved with them.
    ISBN 0-89686-723-4
    1. Cults—United States—Juvenile literature.   2. United States—Religion—
1960–Juvenile literature. [1. Cults.]   I. Title.   II. Series: Facts About
BL2525.S75   1992
291—dc20   91-17774

PHOTO CREDITS

Cover: Alison Blake
Alison Blake: 24, 27, 29
Jeff Greenberg: 4, 6-7, 9, 14-15, 23, 33, 36-37, 39, 41, 43
Samuel Saylor: 19

Copyright © 1992 by Crestwood House, Macmillan Publishing Company

CRESTWOOD HOUSE

Crestwood House   Maxwell Macmillan Canada, Inc.
Macmillan Publishing Company   1200 Eglinton Avenue East
866 Third Avenue   Suite 200
New York, NY 10022   Don Mills, Ontario M3C 3N1

Macmillan Publishing Company is part of the Maxwell Communication Group of Companies.

First edition

Printed in the United States of America

10   9   8   7   6   5   4   3   2   1

CONTENTS

Some young people are introduced to cults at casual meetings.

NO FREE LUNCH

"All I can eat for a dollar? Count me in," Doug said. After a year at college, he was almost broke. A cheap dinner was always welcome. Besides, the Creative Community Project had some pretty interesting ideas. They said their social programs would start a "new age." Doug was eager to lend a hand.

Dinner was good, but Doug was more impressed with the people. Like him, they were concerned about helping others and making the world a better place. They talked about being "pioneers," fighting society's problems.

Everyone was very friendly. Their attention made Doug feel really important. He never suspected that these warm, outgoing people wanted him to join a cult.

After dinner, the group leader spoke about the project—and about God. At first Doug was surprised. Nobody had told him that this was a religious group. And although Doug hadn't come to be preached at, he liked what he heard.

The leader spoke about changing the world and fulfilling God's plan. Everyone in the room paid attention to the speaker. When the speech was over, Doug signed up for a weekend seminar to learn more about these new ideas.

WHAT ARE CULTS?

Doug is one of thousands of young people who join cults each year. The dictionary says a *cult* is any group of people bound together by devotion to a person, belief or set of practices.

Sometimes you hear the word used casually. People talk about the "physical fitness cult" or the "cult" of Elvis Presley. There are even cults of various saints

Many people mistakenly use the word "cult" to describe an unfamiliar religion.

within the Roman Catholic church. All cults have one thing in common: extreme devotion to a person or idea.

The word *cult* comes from the Latin word *cultus,* meaning worship. Many cults are offshoots of major world religions. These cults may seem strange to Americans because their practices are unfamiliar. In fact, many people use the word *cult* to describe any kind of unfamiliar religion.

What do people mean when they call a group a cult? They may think that the group's leaders are fakes. They may find the group's *doctrines*, or beliefs, strange. They may even be afraid of the group because its members dress or behave differently.

Many nontraditional religions are looked down on by mainstream society. But not all cults are destructive or bad.

What makes a cult destructive?

The American Family Foundation says that a *destructive cult* does the following things:

1. manipulates and exploits its members;
2. dictates how members should think, feel and act;
3. claims a special status that sets it apart from mainstream society; and
4. uses *mind control* (*brainwashing*) to recruit people and to keep members obedient.

Mind control takes away a person's ability to make decisions. When a person is no longer able to act inde-

Destructive cults can wear down a person's will by limiting privacy.

pendently because of his or her involvement with a cult, that person has been brainwashed.

How does a cult take control?

"It was very subtle," José Mantos says. He joined a cult when he ran away from home. José was only 17 at the time. "You think you're in control, but you're not."

Every morning José was awakened before dawn. He went to work in a fish-packing factory that the cult owned. All day long, he cleaned and gutted fish.

"There wasn't enough to eat and I couldn't get much sleep," José recalls. "When I wasn't working, I was chanting. I kept repeating things they told me to say. I was so tired and hungry, I couldn't even think straight." By limiting food, sleep and privacy, destructive cults can wear down a person's willpower.

Not all destructive cults are religious. Some are based on the misuse of psychotherapy. Others are get-rich-quick schemes. And some are even political. What destructive cults have in common is that they use deception and mind control.

BRAINWASHING AND BLOODBATHS

The headline shocked Los Angeles on August 9, 1969:

FILM STAR, 4 OTHERS
DEAD IN BLOOD ORGY
SHARON TATE VICTIM IN "RITUAL" MURDERS

Sharon Tate was the pregnant wife of movie director Roman Polanski. Four other bloody bodies littered the grounds of her home in Beverly Hills.

The next night, two other well-to-do victims were murdered in Los Angeles. The killers were members of a cult led by Charles Manson. Manson's followers— called the Family—thought that Manson was Jesus

Christ. They would do anything he asked, even kill innocent people without question.

Manson believed the world was on the brink of *Armageddon*. According to the Bible, Armageddon is the last battle between good and evil. But Manson added a new twist to the biblical prophecy.

He thought that Armageddon would be a violent racial war. Blacks would overthrow whites. In the end, the winners would ask Manson to rule the world for them.

Manson called this revolution Helter Skelter. This was also the name of a popular song by the Beatles. Manson thought that the Beatles' music contained secret messages just for him. He would twist their lyrics to prove his unusual theories.

Besides the Bible and the Beatles, Manson got some of his ideas from a satanic cult called the Process. His ideas were also influenced by the racist policies of Adolf Hitler.

Like Hitler, Manson believed that other races were inferior to whites. He thought that blacks were too ignorant to start Helter Skelter on their own. Manson and the Family would have to show them how.

By brutally murdering rich white victims, Manson hoped that the blame would fall on blacks. This would set off race riots and revolution. Soon Manson and the Family would be asked to take charge.

These beliefs may seem bizarre 20 years later, but Manson had many loyal followers at the time. How did he manage to influence so many people? And how did he get them to kill?

Manson used well-known mind control techniques, including isolation and repetition. The Family lived on a secluded ranch, cut off from society. There were no clocks or newspapers. There were no outside influences or ideas—only Manson and his beliefs.

Manson lectured the Family several times a day. While they ate, he played his guitar and preached about Helter Skelter. Gradually he drummed his ideas into their thoughts.

Manson was always aware of what he was doing. His methods were no accident. In court he stated, "You can convince anybody of anything if you push it at them all of the time."

Drugs were also used to brainwash members. LSD helped "open their minds" to Manson's teachings. It made them more willing to obey. But Manson was always careful to take a smaller dose than the others. He wanted to remain in control.

Manson used drugs, isolation, and repetition to keep control. But his ability to understand members' emotions was most important of all. By sensing and fulfilling their emotional needs, Manson gained their trust.

Most members of Manson's Family were basically unhappy. In different ways, they were all looking for acceptance. Some had family problems. Many were runaways or dropouts. Because of this Manson was able to "psych out" their problems and give them a sense of belonging. In return, they let him dominate their lives.

Paul Watkins was Manson's second-in-command for a time. He remembers how complete the mind control was. "I lived with Charlie for one year straight," he explains. "I *became* Charlie. There was nothing left of me anymore." Charles Manson had destroyed Watkins's personality and replaced it with his own ideas.

At least nine vicious murders have been linked to the Manson Family. But some people think that the cult may have killed as many as 40 people. Today many members are still in prison. Manson is serving a life sentence in a California jail. Several requests for parole have been denied.

THE CULT OF PERSONALITY

Destructive cults often have a certain type of leader. He or she is usually self-appointed and all-powerful. Members may be used to promote the leader's power or wealth.

Some destructive cults have more than one leader. They may claim to run the cult in the name of a dead leader, but they usually have their own interests at heart.

Bhagwan Shree Rajneesh was a typical cult leader. He started from humble beginnings as a spiritual

Some cult leaders are driven by power and wealth. Bhagwan Shree Rajneesh was known for his power—and his fleet of Rolls-Royces.

teacher, or *guru*, in Poona, India. Between 1981 and 1985, he had 20,000 Western followers and a huge ranch in Oregon. The ranch was a *commune*—a settlement where people try to live together in harmony.

Rajneesh's followers were struck by their leader's *charisma*—the power of his personality. Many say that he was able to give them an amazing sense of unconditional love. Others were impressed by his teachings. All agree that he was a very convincing speaker.

Rajneesh's personality was so strong that his disciples "surrendered" to him. They thought that if they gave him total control of their lives, they would find true peace and enlightenment.

But there was more to Rajneesh than charisma. He was driven by a desire for power and wealth. Having loyal followers and a fleet of 85 Rolls-Royces helped him meet those needs. The needs were so great that they drove Rajneesh and his aides to excess.

Psychiatrists call people like Rajneesh *megalomaniacs*. Megalomaniacs are people with a type of mental disorder. They think they are special and exalted above other people. They may think that this gives them special status and that they don't need to follow the rules.

Rajneesh and his aides broke many rules. In 1985 Rajneesh was sent back to India because he had broken immigration laws. One year later, his main aide was found guilty of attempted murder, assault, arson and wiretapping.

MONEY-MAKERS?

Pam Chambers was on her way to visit her sister in Tulsa. She was walking through the airport when two cute guys stopped her.

"How are you?" one of them asked. He was so friendly, Pam wondered if he knew her. His blue eyes sparkled as he smiled.

The other guy handed Pam a pamphlet. "This will tell you about the path to peace and enlightenment," he said.

Then the young man asked Pam to make a donation to their group.

Although Pam gave them some change, she felt used. She had stopped to talk because the guys were attractive. But they had lost interest as soon as they got her money.

Cults may promise enlightenment and inner peace. But many cults have been accused of being money-making schemes. Some cults profit from the cheap labor of members. Other cults charge huge fees for seminars and lectures that teach the group's beliefs. Still others convince members to hand over everything they own. A new member may be asked to donate all of his or her money and property to the group.

Income is tax free if a cult is classified as a religious organization. Under federal law, religious groups don't have to pay taxes. As a result, a cult's leaders are free to control large sums of money.

Religious groups don't have to file financial statements with the Internal Revenue Service. This way, no one really knows how much money they make—or where all that money goes.

MOON'S EMPIRE

The Reverend Sun Myung Moon is a well-known cult leader. Born in Korea in 1920, he studied engineering and was a dockworker as a young man. He founded the Unification Church in 1954.

Members of the Unification Church are often called *Moonies*. Their *doctrine*—or set of beliefs—is loosely based on Christian teachings. However, it suggests that the Reverend Moon—not Jesus—is the true savior. In court testimony, Moon has even claimed to have spoken with Jesus, Buddha and Moses.

The Reverend Moon brought his church to the United States in 1971. Before long, he had turned it into a huge money-making empire. Today the Unification Church owns successful businesses in all 50 states and in many foreign countries.

"Moonies" sell candy and flowers on the streets, bringing in over $25 million a year. However, sellers rarely tell customers that their money goes to the Unification Church and the Reverend Moon.

The Unification Church also owns art galleries, a drug company and food-processing plants. And it operates factories in Korea that produce grenades and parts for M-16 rifles.

One way the Reverend Moon cuts costs is by using church members as workers. Some "Moonies" work long hours in church businesses. Then they turn their wages over to the cult. The Unification Church says that turning over wages is a matter of individual choice. After all, many people choose to give money to their churches.

Reverend Sun Myung Moon was convicted by the government for lying on his personal income tax returns.

But Moon's critics think he's more interested in making money than in saving souls. By setting up a church, the Reverend Moon is able to keep most of the profits from his financial empire. Should this be allowed?

The government took a close look at Moon's finances in 1982. He was convicted of conspiracy to avoid taxes—lying on his personal income tax returns. Moon was jailed for over a year, but his church businesses continue to flourish.

MONEY WORSHIP?

"I was in pretty bad shape when I saw the ad on TV," Adam explained. "I'd just broken up with my girlfriend. I was depressed. I was mad at the world. But the ad talked about solving my problems. It said that the answers were in a book called *Dianetics*."

The ad Adam had seen was for a book by L. Ron Hubbard. A former writer, Hubbard was the founder of a cult called Scientology.

Adam bought the book. "I read it," he said, "and it helped me. But I wanted to know more." So Adam called the Scientology office in his town. "They told me about a course in Dianetics. It sounded good—until they told me the price. Fifteen hundred dollars! I just couldn't afford it."

L. Ron Hubbard is the founder of a cult called Scientology.

Many cults raise money by making people pay for instruction. The Way International is an evangelical Christian cult that takes in large sums of money. They charge from $200 to $10,000 for a course called "Power for Abundant Living." And members of the Church Universal and Triumphant pay thousands of dollars to hear taped lectures by their leader, Elizabeth Clare Prophet.

Is spiritual knowledge worth all that money? Should people have to pay for enlightenment?

"I think it was worth it," says 19-year-old Monica Farmer. Monica has paid thousands of dollars for cult lectures and retreats. "Nobody made me pay the money. I did it because I wanted to learn more."

Where did Monica's money go? "To our leaders," she says. "They need money to live on, just like you and me. My moneys means that they can concentrate on spiritual things and not worry about paying the bills."

Cults aren't the only groups that ask for money from their members. Political parties ask for campaign funds. Charities need money to support good works. And all religions need money to pay their clergy and maintain church buildings.

Many faiths, such as the Mormons, *tithe* their members. The church asks each member to donate one-tenth of his or her total income. And many Jewish temples require worshipers to pay an annual membership fee.

How is this different from asking members to pay to find out more about a group's beliefs?

22 *Many churches and temples ask worshipers to give money to their institutions.*

HARE KRISHNA, HARE KRISHNA

One of the most visible cults in America is *Hare Krishna*. It is a modern branch of one of the world's oldest religions, Hinduism. The group's full name is the International Society for Krishna Consciousness. It is also known by the initials ISKCON.

The group was founded in 1966 by a man called Swami Prabhupada. ISKCON has been run by a committee of 11 people since the swami's death in 1977.

Hare Krishna is a branch of one of the world's oldest religions, Hinduism.

Today Hare Krishna claims to have thousands of followers all over the world.

"Hare Krishna" is a *Sanskrit* phrase. It means "O Lord Krishna." It is also the first line of the group's special *mantra*—mystic words used in prayer and meditation.

In Hinduism, Krishna is a human form of the great god *Vishnu*. The Hare Krishnas believe that devotion to Krishna will bring them enlightenment and union with God. Chanting the mantra is a key part of their devotion.

Groups of enthusiastic young Krishnas used to be a common sight on street corners across the country. They chanted the mantra and played drums and cymbals to attract new members to the group.

Twenty-five-year-old Janine is a member of Hare Krishna. She chants the mantra hundreds of times a day. "At first I felt sort of silly," she says. "But after a while, I felt peaceful. At one with the universe. It's an amazing feeling of being at one with God."

Janine's mother doesn't see things the same way. "They make their members chant for hours. It's all a trick to control their minds." Besides, Janine's mother had read that two Hare Krishnas had been convicted of murdering a drug dealer. What had Janine gotten into?

"My mom was nervous because the Krishnas are different," Janine explains. "Some members wear long robes. We chant in a language she doesn't understand. And some of the men shave their heads. My mother is pretty old-fashioned. She just doesn't know what to make of us."

But what about the problems with the law?

"It's true that two guys were convicted of murder," Janine admits. "But they were just a couple of bad apples. You can't judge the whole group based on the actions of a few men."

RELIGIOUS FREEDOM

In 1982 the people of Moundsville, West Virginia, agreed with Janine's mother. They objected to the Krishnas' unusual life-style. And they were upset when the group set up a commune near their town.

Who were these strangers who woke up at four in the morning to work on the commune? Why didn't they drink coffee or alcohol? And why did they abstain from sex? It all seemed very strange to the people of Moundsville.

Prominent citizens like the sheriff expressed their disapproval of the Krishnas. "When the Founding Fathers wrote about freedom of religion, they didn't have people like this in mind," he said.

The sheriff was wrong. Freedom of religion applies to all Americans. It is the reason our forefathers first came to America. The Pilgrims were escaping religious persecution in England when they set sail on the *Mayflower*.

They dreamed of a land where they wouldn't be punished for their beliefs.

The *First Amendment* to the U.S. Constitution ensures that all Americans can enjoy the freedom that the Pilgrims dreamed of. It promises that "Congress shall make no law respecting an establishment of religion or prohibiting the free exercise thereof."

This means that all people are free to choose how and what they will worship.

Many Americans choose not to worship. The First Amendment protects that right, as well. Others choose to be Baptists, Mormons, Muslims, or Jews. Still others choose to worship 35,000-year-old spirits or space aliens. Those are their rights.

Groups of enthusiastic young Krishnas can sometimes be seen on street corners. They play music and chant the mantra.

Because we have religious freedom, many Americans never think about it. We may take it for granted. But we only have to look to other countries to realize how privileged we are.

Until recently Soviet citizens could not worship freely. The Soviet Union was an *atheist* nation. Government policy denied the existence of God.

Often Soviet people who chose to worship were persecuted by the government. They could be prevented from getting an education or good jobs. And religious people were not allowed to work for the government.

Fourteen-year-old Rachel has some strong views on religious freedom. "I don't like the views or practices of some cults. But I think that all Americans should be free to believe what they want," she says.

Rachel's grandparents had to flee Germany in the 1930s. Because they were Jews, they were no longer safe in their homeland. "They were lucky to get out," Rachel adds. "Six million Jews were killed in German concentration camps during World War Two. If we start criticizing one religious group, who knows where it could lead?"

BLIND FAITH

America discovered just how dangerous some cults could be in 1978. More than 900 people were found dead in Guyana, South America. The incident became known as the *Jonestown* massacre.

Americans have the right to worship almost anything they choose: God, Jesus, spirits or space aliens.

Why did hundreds of people kill themselves—and their children?

The Peoples Temple was a cult that began in northern California. It was founded by the Reverend Jim Jones. In the 1970s the group left the United States and moved to the jungles of South America. They started their own community, named Jonestown after their leader.

The mass suicide was ordered by the Reverend Jones. And the members were so devoted to Jones that they followed his command. Hundreds of people drank cups of Kool-Aid laced with poison.

The deaths in Jonestown made many people wonder about cults—and about personal freedom. Members of the Peoples Temple didn't have much personal freedom. The Reverend Jones told members how they should live in the commune. In the end, he told them how they should die.

Did the members of the Peoples Temple give up too much personal freedom in their search for religious fulfillment?

Many other cults limit personal freedom, too. The Reverend Moon arranges marriages for his followers. And Bhagwan Shree Rajneesh did not let his disciples leave the ranch or make phone calls without permission.

Of course, many mainstream religions also tell their followers how to live. The Catholic church has firm teachings on abortion, birth control and divorce. Orthodox Jews follow complex dietary laws. They also have strict rules about working on the Sabbath.

But do these restrictions limit personal freedom? How are they different from the control exercised by destructive cults? And how much control is *too* much control?

"WE WANT OUR DAUGHTER BACK!"

Jim and Elsa Miller didn't like the changes they were seeing in their 21-year-old daughter, Barbara. Six months earlier she had dropped out of college and joined a cult.

Barbara had moved out of the school dorm. She was now sharing a house with cult members. She spent all her time working in a cult business. She even refused to speak to her parents.

Jim and Elsa missed their daughter. They wanted to get "the old Barbara" back.

The Millers went to court to get temporary custody of their daughter. They had to prove that Barb was *mentally incompetent*—that she could not make her own decisions. To do that they hired a specialist named Brian to testify in court.

Brian is a *deprogrammer.* He provides special counseling for cult members. By talking with them, he helps them to break free from destructive cults. Over time, cult members are able to regain *critical thought*—the

ability to make reasonable decisions of their own free will.

On the stand, Brian told the judge about the mind control methods used by Barb's cult. Barb was not allowed much sleep. She had to work long hours. And she didn't get enough food to eat. The judge ruled that Barb was not in a position to control her own life. Her parents were granted temporary custody.

Now that they had legal control of Barb, the Millers could get her into counseling. At first, Barb wanted no part of it. The cult had taught her not to trust anyone outside the group. But as Brian began to point out how the cult had mistreated her, Barb reconsidered.

"I still had lots of spiritual questions," Barb says. "But I saw that no one has *all* the answers—not even the cult. Now I understand why my parents stepped in. They were worried about me. I'm glad they got me out."

KIDNAPPED

The Millers chose one of the few legal routes available to families of cult members. They were lucky. It is difficult to prove mental incompetence. Many frustrated families are not able to get custody. Sometimes they go outside the law to get their children back.

"I wanted my son back," Tina Green explained. "The courts were no help. Since Colin was an adult, they told

Parents and teens often disagree about cults and cult practices.

us we had no right to interfere. But even though he was 22, Colin was still my son. I couldn't let those people ruin his life."

Colin's parents wanted to help him break free from the cult. They decided to kidnap him. As he walked to work one day, two men grabbed him from behind. At first, Colin thought he was being mugged. Then he heard his father saying, "Relax, Colin. We just want to talk with you."

Colin's parents locked him in their basement for a few weeks. They brought in a deprogrammer named Jack to work with their son.

Jack spent a lot of time talking to Colin. But Colin wanted nothing to do with his parents' scheme. He fought with Jack. He tried to escape. He wanted to return to the Unification Church. "What about my rights?" he screamed.

Forced deprogramming can be a very expensive way to get a loved one back. Top deprogrammers may charge $10,000 or more for their services. Forced deprogramming usually involves kidnapping and restraining a person against his or her will. It is illegal in most states.

The courts treat deprogrammers like Jack the same as they would any criminal. One deprogrammer named Ted Patrick was sentenced to a year in prison. Patrick was found guilty of planning a kidnapping. Since then, fewer cult members have been taken by force.

The court rulings have given deprogramming a bad

name. For that reason, specialists like Brian prefer to call themselves *"exit counselors."* They don't want people to confuse them with deprogrammers who break the law.

Exit counselors only work with cult members who are willing to talk. These counselors do not kidnap members. Good exit counselors do not force their own views on cult members. They simply present options.

GETTING GRANDMA BACK

"Don't tell me what to do with my money!" shouted Jake's grandma. "I can give money to whoever I please. I'm not senile yet, you know."

Jake's dad was furious. Grandma had just sent a big check to a group called the Golden Brigade. "Don't you realize these people are fakes?" he insisted. "They're not a real church. They just want your money."

Jake's grandmother disagreed. "The Golden Brigade is a terrific group. They pay attention to me and come to visit—which is more than you do! It can get awfully lonely being an old lady, you know. Besides, my contribution will help their missionaries overseas."

Jake wasn't sure if the Golden Brigade really had any missionaries overseas. He doubted it was true. But he

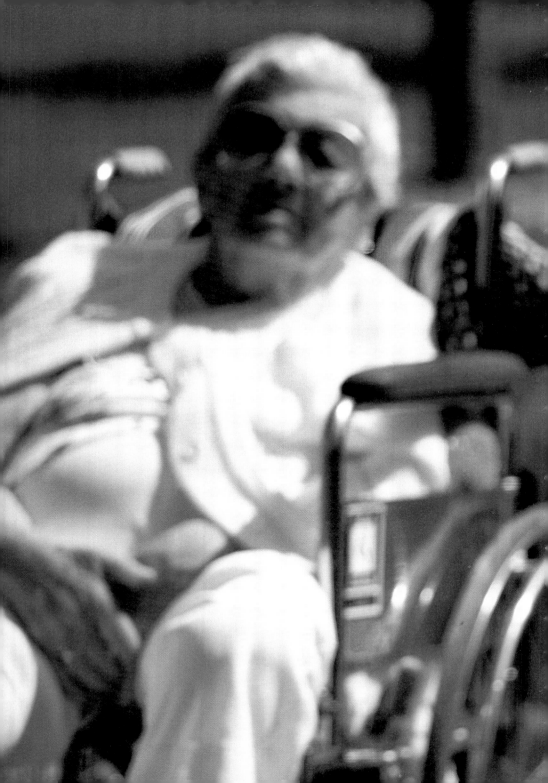

Senior citizens are likely cult targets. They may be lonely or isolated, and many cults offer "reach out" programs.

did think that Grandma was old enough to make up her own mind.

"As long as she's happy, I don't really care what she does with her money," Jake says. "But my dad thinks we need a deprogrammer. I think we just need to make sure Grandma knows that we care about her, that she's part of our family."

OLD TACTICS, NEW TARGETS

Senior citizens may not seem like probable cult members. But cults are having a tough time recruiting young people. According to *sociologists*—people who study society's behavior—young people today are less interested in spirituality than young people were in the past. Instead they're concerned about careers, education and their future. Cults have had to look elsewhere for new recruits.

The elderly are prime targets for several reasons. First, there are a lot of senior citizens. In fact, women over 65 are the fastest-growing group in America. And with death approaching, many elderly people begin to think about life after death.

Destructive cults have a special interest in the elderly.

Young people today are not as interested in spirituality as they have been in the past. Instead they are concerned with education, careers and their futures.

Unlike younger people, senior citizens may have large sums of money in the bank. And as Reginald Alev of the Cult Awareness Network says, "Cults go where the money is."

Some cults make special efforts to recruit the elderly. Cult members go to nursing homes and retirement centers and speak to the residents. Some cult recruiters pose as live-in helpers. Others may offer to visit shut-ins or drive them to appointments.

The Unification Church has a unit called the Orange Blossom Corps, which tries to "reach out" to seniors.

And the Way International has formed the Sunset Corps for all its elderly members.

Senior citizens may feel lonely or isolated, especially if they've lost a spouse. Religion can be a great comfort to them. Television preachers have reached out to these people for years—and profited from it. Today destructive cults are trying to do the same thing.

NEW AGE OR NONSENSE?

A new trend in spirituality is spreading across America: *New Age*. New Age isn't a religion with a leader and a doctrine. Instead it's a movement that blends beliefs from various world religions.

Healing crystals, self-help groups and soothing New Age music are popular New Age trends. Many "New Agers" also believe in the occult and psychic abilities. And many believe in *reincarnation*—that a person's soul is "reborn" in another body after death.

New Age beliefs and practices provide inspiration and a spiritual experience for some people. But some aspects, such as *channeling,* can have as much control over followers as a destructive cult.

Many New Agers believe that humans can communicate with dead spirits. These spirits send messages through people known as channelers, or mediums. Skeptics think that channeling is a fake. They say that channelers just pretend to receive spirit messages.

J. Z. Knight is a well-known channeler. This Washington housewife says that Ramtha, a 35,000-year-old spirit, speaks through her. Ramtha's messages talk about life, death, peace and happiness.

Followers have spent thousands of dollars each on Ramtha tapes, videos and seminars. They are eager to learn the wisdom of the ages from this spirit. Ms. Knight has made a lot of money passing on Ramtha's messages.

The tarot is one element in the popular New Age movement.

Channelers like Ms. Knight often claim to be the only source of divine truth. Their followers believe that the answers to life's big questions can only come from these spirits. This can have a very powerful hold on believers and their spiritual lives.

But what happens when a channeler starts offering more than just spiritual advice?

Pam is a businesswoman in her thirties who was drawn to J. Z. Knight and Ramtha. She paid over $5,000, hoping for spiritual enlightenment. When Ramtha predicted that natural disasters would strike the rest of the country, Pam even considered selling her house and moving to Washington State to be safe.

Another time Ramtha told believers to invest in J. Z. Knight's expensive Arabian horses. Many did so without question. Later some members complained and the authorities began to investigate. Ms. Knight gave back the money in order to avoid a scandal.

Did J. Z. Knight use her followers' faith to her own advantage? Was she manipulating them so that she could get rich? How is this like a destructive cult?

THE BEST DEFENSE

Cults have changed a lot since the Jonestown tragedy. The horrible images of dead bodies lying in the jungle

A good way to avoid becoming a victim is to ask questions. Cult awareness groups can help you get a better understanding of different types of cults.

alerted the nation to the dangers of destructive cults.

Jonestown also inspired a backlash against nontraditional religious groups. Many groups were labeled cults simply because they weren't familiar Christian or Jewish faiths.

Destructive cults still exist in America. Your best defense is a strong offense. To avoid becoming a victim, be a questioner. Don't accept everything you hear as true. Ask questions. Gather information. Then make up your own mind. Don't let anyone else make it up for you.

FOR MORE INFORMATION

For more information about cults and cultism, please contact:

The Cult Awareness Network (CAN)
National Office
2421 West Pratt Blvd., Suite 1173
Chicago, IL 60645
(312) 267-7777

CAN is a national, nonprofit group that can refer you to anticult groups in your area. CAN is concerned about illegal and unethical activities of destructive cults, especially mind control. However, they do not judge the doctrines or beliefs of these groups.

CAN provides exit counseling to help cult members regain critical thinking and reenter mainstream society. The group also supports all legal efforts to restore cult members to freedom of action and choice.

Other sources of information:

Jewish Board of Family & Children's Services
24-Hour Cult Clinic Hotline
1651 Third Avenue
New York, NY 10128
(212) 860-8533

B'nai B'rith Cult Program
1640 Rhode Island Avenue, NW
Washington, D.C. 20036
(202) 857-6600

The Jewish community has been very involved in the anticult movement. Figures for some cult groups show that as many as half their members are Jewish. By comparison, Jews make up only about 3 percent of the American population. You don't have to be Jewish to call this hotline to or contact B'nai B'rith. The services are available to everyone, regardless of religious background.

American Bar Association
Sub-Committee on Cult-Related Litigation
750 North Lake Shore Drive
Chicago, IL 60611
(312) 988-5662

This group of lawyers can provide information on lawsuits involving cults and on illegal activities by cults.

GLOSSARY/INDEX

ARMAGEDDON 11—*The battle that will occur at the end of the world between the forces of good and evil. Armageddon is prophesied in the Book of Revelation, the last book of the Bible.*

ATHEIST 27—*A person who denies the existence of God.*

BRAINWASHING 8–9, 12—*Mind control; systematically replacing a person's established ideas with a cult's beliefs.*

CHANNELING 40–42—*Communicating with dead spirits through a medium called a channeler.*

CHARISMA 16—*The power of personality.*

COMMUNE 16, 26, 30—*A settlement where people try to live together in harmony. Usually all belongings and property are shared.*

CRITICAL THOUGHT 33—*The ability to make reasonable judgments and decisions of one's own free will.*

CULT 5, 8–10, 11, 13, 17, 19, 21–22, 24, 28, 30, 31, 33, 34, 35, 38, 39, 43, 44–45—*Any group of people bound together by devotion to a person, belief system or set of practices.*

DEPROGRAMMER 31, 34–35, 38—*A counselor who works with cult members to help them break away from destructive cults and regain critical thought. Forced deprogramming may involve kidnapping and restraining a person against his or her will.*

46

DESTRUCTIVE CULT 8–9, 10, 13, 31, 38, 40, 42–43, 44—*A cult that deceives or manipulates its members or uses mind control techniques.*

DOCTRINE 8, 18, 40, 44—*A belief that is taught and held as true.*

EXIT COUNSELOR 35, 44—*A deprogrammer who uses only legal means to help cult members regain critical thought.*

FIRST AMENDMENT 27—*The part of the U.S. Constitution that guarantees freedom of religion in the United States.*

GURU 16—*A spiritual teacher. In the Hindi language, guru means "one who leads a disciple from darkness into the light."*

HARE KRISHNA 24–25—*Means "O Lord Krishna" in the Sanskrit language. Familiar name for the International Society for Krishna Consciousness (ISKCON), which believes that devotion to Krishna can bring enlightenment*

JONESTOWN 30, 42—*Commune in Guyana, South America, where over 900 followers of the Reverend Jim Jones and the Peoples Temple committed mass suicide in 1978.*

KRISHNA 25, 26—*In Hinduism, a human form of the god Vishnu. Members of the Hare Krishna religion are sometimes called Krishnas.*

MANTRA 26—*Mystic words used in prayer and meditation.*

MEDIUM 40—*A person who claims to communicate*

with dead spirits and then reveals their messages to others.

MEGALOMANIAC 16—*A mentally disordered person who believes that he or she is great or exalted above other people.*

MENTAL INCOMPETENCE 31, 33—*The inability to make rational decisions.*

MIND CONTROL 8–9, 10, 12, 13, 33, 44—*Brainwashing; destruction of critical thought by techniques such as deprivation of food, sleep and privacy.*

MOONIE 18–19—*Slang name for a member of the Unification Church of the Reverend Sun Myung Moon.*

NEW AGE 40—*A new movement that blends beliefs from Eastern and Western religions.*

REINCARNATION 40—*The belief that a person's soul is "reborn" in another body after death.*

SANSKRIT 25—*The main written language of India.*

SOCIOLOGISTS 38—*People who study society's behavior.*

TITHE 22—*A tenth of a person's income, donated to a religious group.*

VISHNU 26—*Hindu god considered to be the main god and savior by some worshipers. Others consider Vishnu to be one of three main gods.*